10
Radiant
IDEAS

10
Radiant
IDEAS

Awaken your passion for living consciously

A BIG HEART
Miracles Study Guide by
Karen Anne Bentley

Big Heart Books
Sudbury, Massachusetts

Published by Big Heart Books
P. O. Box 909
Sudbury, MA 01776

Phone: 866-UPLIFTS   (875-4387) toll free
Fax: 866-UPLIFTU (875-4388) toll free
E-mail: info@big-heart.com

Edited by Robin Quinn
Cover and Interior Design, and Typesetting by
Desktop Miracles, Inc., Stowe, VT

Publisher's Cataloguing-in-Publication Data
Big Heart
10 radiant ideas – awaken your passion for living consciously – Karen Anne Bentley – Sudbury, MA; Big Heart Books, 2001

ISBN 0-9666967-2-7

Portions of *A Course In Miracles*® © copyright 1975, 1992, 1996 reprinted by permission of the *Foundation for A Course In Miracles, Inc.*® (www.facim.org). All rights reserved.

A Course In Miracles® is a registered trademark of the *Foundation for A Course In Miracles*®.

"The ideas represented herein are the personal interpretation and understanding of the author and are not necessarily endorsed by the copyright holder of *A Course In Miracles*®."

All quotations from *A Course In Miracles*® can be located using the following reference system:

	ACIM	Acronym for *A Course In Miracles*®
	ACIM-T	Indicates quote is from the Text.
	ACIM-W	Indicates quote is from the Workbook.
	ACIM-M	Indicates quote is from the Manual for Teachers.
Example:	ACIM-T.123	Refers you to page 123 in Text.

Dedication

To the two Bills,
who have always been my inspiration.

Thank you

*Love is the way I walk
in gratitude.* **ACIM-W.372**

This is to express my great appreciation (in alphabetical order, of course) to Moira Collins, Tony D'Andrea, Jill Geller, Cathy Glick, Cristalle Maye, and Glenn Munyan, the people who studied and discussed *A Course In Miracles*® with me during 1999 and 2000. Your presence and interest prompted me to explain these radiant ideas in a way that can be easily understood and applied by others. I am grateful now and always.

I wish also to acknowledge the contribution made by Kenneth Wapnick, PhD, of the Foundation for A Course In Miracles®, for his extensive collection of work explaining Course concepts. I am enormously thankful to Dr. Wapnick for his review and critique of an earlier draft of this book. Even though all of his suggestions for changes were not incorporated, Dr. Wapnick's logic and questions helped me to clarify, complete, and strengthen my message.

And finally, many thanks to Robin Quinn, editor extraordinaire! Robin helped me to organize, refine, and polish this book, and to make it shine like a beacon of light. I am grateful to be the recipient of Robin's keen insights and talents.

XXOO,

Karen Anne Bentley

Big Heart

Truth can only be recognized
and need only be recognized.

ACIM-T.117

Table of Contents

Heaven is chosen consciously. The choice
cannot be made until alternatives are accurately
seen and understood. **ACIM-W.265**

Foreword

10 Radiant Ideas will grab your attention and hold it from the first page to the last. That is because Karen Anne Bentley has captured, with her simple yet power-packed ideas, the formula for healing. Whether it is **A Course In Miracles**® or another path towards awakening that you walk, the principles and suggestions found in her *10 Radiant Ideas* will hasten your journey.

To meet Karen is to experience an energetic presence that pulls you into her vitality and love. While reading her book, I felt as though I were with her in person, interacting with deep conversation about life and its meaning. Karen's writing is intensely personal and speaks of powerful concepts like "The value of seeing your own worth is incomprehensible," or "A decision reached with the help of God becomes an expression of fullness," or "Do you want life or a dream of fear?" I could go on and on. In fact, as I got deeper into her book, I realized that I had underlined something on almost every page.

Ideas like these meet the challenge of any thinker, writer, and teacher, for these are invitations to the mind for acceptance, healing, and change. If you truly want to undergo the transformation from fear to faith, from pain to pleasure, from darkness to light, then treat yourself to this book. There's a gem in every chapter. You will not be able to put it down until you have reached the end whereupon you will discover the true meaning of "The Lord's Prayer." *10 Radiant Ideas* is on my "must read" list. I suspect it will be on yours too!!

JOHN NAGY
A Course In Miracles® Teacher and Author
Chairman of Quest Foundation

Introduction

*Meaningful seeking is consciously undertaken,
consciously organized, and consciously
directed. The goal must be formulated clearly
and kept in mind.* **ACIM-T.66**

*An untrained mind can accomplish
nothing.* **ACIM-W.1**

onsciousness means you are aware of who you are, what you want, and what you're either doing or not doing to get it. The purpose of this book is to introduce you, the reader, to a radiant "thought system" for becoming more conscious of your divine identity, and for inspiring you to extract more meaning, usefulness, and joy from your current life experience.

Awareness is one of those simple concepts that sounds easy, but isn't. We all think we know what we're doing, but mostly we're on automatic. Our internal robot allows us to go to sleep and coast through life in an uncreative, habitual way, without paying very much attention to what we're doing or why we're doing it. The process of waking up and becoming free starts by *paying attention*. Attention is keenest when learning a new skill or when a crisis forces you to abandon tired, old ways that no longer work.

> Any activity done with consciousness can serve to increase awareness, even public speaking. Toastmasters is a truly wonderful non-profit organization that teaches people of any age or background to speak in public with confidence and clarity. One of the basic skills they teach is how to talk without relying on um's and ah's to fill up space. Many novice speakers litter their presentations with unconscious um's and ah's. Other toastmasters in the group help the new speaker to develop awareness by counting the number of times one of these sounds is used. This "noticing activity" forces the new speaker to pay closer attention to what he or she is doing. The speaker cannot exploit the potential to self-correct until he or she has awareness of the um/ah speaking habit. *Change of any kind is not possible without awareness of what you're doing or not doing.*

The great benefit of coming in contact with a new existential thought system is that it forces you to examine your current beliefs about God, the nature of the world, and the purpose of your life. *The act of looking squarely and directly at your thoughts enables you to assess whether they're serving you in the most constructive and uplifting way. You are then able to make a conscious, informed choice. You can keep your current ideas, you can continue to evaluate them, or you can change your way of thinking.*

Some people are afraid of being exposed to new or radically different ideas, but there is nothing to be afraid of. Nothing can happen to you and nothing will happen to you unless you choose it. You are simply being open to the possibility of changing your mind about your current beliefs. This puts you in the driver's seat. Beliefs must make complete logical sense, or it is your duty to reject them.

Your beliefs about God and the purpose of existence are very important. This is because your beliefs drive your decisions. Your decisions drive your attention and your behavior. And your behavior determines your happiness. There we are again, back to happiness. Why is it so hard to be happy, especially when so many of us have followed the prescription for happiness so carefully? Most of us are doing everything we think we're supposed to do. For instance, you may identify with many of the following ways in which you have followed the program for happiness:

> I have every conceivable convenience.
> I have constant entertainment.
> I have instant information.
> I have supportive friends.
> I have a beautiful family.
> I have a decent job.

I pay my bills.
I take care of my health.
I work on fulfilling my dreams.
I am a responsible caretaker and citizen.

With all this, how is it possible that we are still unhappy? Still empty?

"It must be me," you think. "I must be doing something wrong." Or "it must be the people I'm going through life with. I would be happy except for the miserable, difficult, unfair people I'm with. If only I had better parents. If only my spouse were kind." We like to blame ourselves and each other. No one, however, looks at the underlying program and system of beliefs that we've been taught, that we have reinforced, and embellished since our arrival on this planet. This thought system directs our attention to people, things, and events outside of ourselves for happiness. It does not direct us within. Herein lies the clue.

Everything external is uncertain, constantly changing, and ultimately temporary. Change is very exciting and distracting, but it's also a block to happiness. Changing conditions require constant adjustment. The prospect of change also produces *fear* because there's always the chance that a so-called good situation might end or a so-called bad situation might get worse. One minute conditions are the way you want them, the next minute they're not. It's exasperating! Most of us devote at least 99% of our attention to our ever-changing conditional existence. So it's no wonder that we are unhappy! Very few of us devote even 1% of our attention to that which never changes, *the silent self within.* This silent self is sure, immutable, holy, and eternal. *The best way to experience unshakeable happiness is to begin to focus attention on what is changeless and eternal.* When you pay attention to that which does not change, you become less fearful and more happy. And this happiness is unshakeable because there are no variable conditions that will diminish it or take it away.

This book introduces you to *10 Radiant Ideas* that lead to the recognition of yourself as holy, changeless, and eternal. The ideas are based on **A Course In Miracles®,** perhaps the most profound, practical, and uplifting spiritual book of our time. Big Heart provides this brief interpretation of the Course for your inspiration and convenience. Keep in mind, however, that all interpreters are subject to errors in omission and translation. Therefore, if you have any doubts or questions, go directly to the source and check for yourself.

Are there other spiritual ideas worth considering? Of course! Other paths? Of course. There are many. This is not intended to be a complete or exclusive orientation. Rather, it's an overview of an extraordinary thought system that's accessible to all, from the seeker who is mildly curious, to one who is serious about rediscovering holiness and living in a way so as to demonstrate the devine.

- If the thoughts in your mind are making you miserable, and you want to change them, consider **A Course In Miracles®.** *Your mind will be changed.*

- If you want to like what you see when you look in the mirror, consider *A Course In Miracles*®. *Your perspective will be sweetened.*
- If you need a miracle or a healing in your life, consider *A Course In Miracles*®. *Miracles are your birthright. Become a miracle worker.*
- If you want to find the love that's in yourself and others, consider *A Course In Miracles*®. *This is the path to, and of, love.*
- If you want to connect with God and to meet the formless, free spirit of Jesus, consider *A Course In Miracles*®. *You will meet Jesus in a new and personal way. He is there.*

A Course In Miracles® is completely harmless. It cannot hurt you in any way. It can only help. Go to the library, browse through the Course, and check it out for yourself. Look for it in the inspirational, religious, or new age section.

God is only love

Love is extension. To withhold the
smallest gift is not to know love's purpose.
Love offers everything forever.
Hold back but one belief, one offering, and
love is gone, because you asked a substitute
to take its place. **ACIM-T.499**

No law the world obeys can help you grasp
love's meaning. **ACIM-W.230**

he term "God" is used to describe our Creator, the Source of all life. *God's love is wholly benevolent and wholly good.* His love is immutable, and eternal. It never changes for any reason. *It is not dependent on any conditions.* It does not matter, for example, whether God's love is recognized and returned by his creations. His light is not dimmed or diminished in any way because we do not see it. His love is not devalued because we do not want it. His love cannot be stopped because we do not believe in Him. God's love constantly extends outward and in all directions into infinity. It cannot be contained, limited, or restricted in any way. His love is completely harmless and wholly without any cruelty, negativity, hate, or destruction. It is not possible for God to be angry, judgmental, punitive, or rejecting because these are limits on love.

It's helpful to think of God's love as being like the sun. The sun's light shines on all things, regardless of their condition or function. It shines on all people, regardless of how those people behave or are valued by society. For example, the sun would shine equally on a Charles Manson and a Mother Teresa. Society judges someone like Manson to be bad and evil and someone like Mother Teresa is judged as saintly and good. But the sun does not judge. Therefore, it does not apportion more light to one and less to another. It just shines freely because its nature is to shine. The sun shines continually without any conditions or limits. It doesn't stop shining because we don't praise it or worship it. It doesn't stop shining because we don't believe in it. It doesn't stop shining because our vision is blocked by a cloud or by the night. It doesn't stop shining because we don't reciprocate with a return of light.

The sun does not ask for anything. Absolutely nothing has to be done to receive the sun's shining light. There is no payment or obligation required. Promises or bargains do not have to be made. Rituals do not have to be performed. Sacrifice of any kind is not required. Prayers or the absence of prayers will not inspire the sun to shine more or less light. Nothing can be said or done that will change the sun's eternal, radiant, expansive nature. The sun cannot be anything but what it is. It can never not be the sun.

Like the sun, God's love is all-powerful. It is infinite. It is always maximal strength, and it is conscious. *Infinite* means there is no end to it. It always and forever IS. *Maximal strength* means that his power cannot be conflicted, opposed, or weakened in any way. His power is not tentative, intermittent, whimsical, constricted, or blocked. These would be limitations on power, and God's power is not limited. *Conscious* means that God's power is on purpose, deliberate, and intentional.

Most importantly, God's love is not special. No being receives more or less love than any other being. Specialness is based on the presence of a particular condition or behavior, and is dependent on a judgment of worthiness. Dependencies, conditions, and/or judgments are limits on love, and are therefore not possible. God's love is perfectly ordinary, perfectly available, and perfectly equal for all his creations. Every being is worthy. No one is excluded or rejected for any reason.

Why is it critically important to recognize that God is love and only love?

- It is not possible to make the decision to go toward something you are afraid of. If you think that God is fearsome or vengeful, you will be afraid of Him.

- If you think that God is capable of sacrificing his children, harming his children, or that he wants to punish his children to prove his omnipotence, you will be afraid of Him.

- If you think that God judges and extracts retribution from his children for their badness, you will be afraid of Him.

- If you think that God's love is special, you will not feel worthy enough to receive it. This leads to fear of rejection and to bargaining with God. You will think that God requires you to do something, anything, to become eligible or worthy of His love.

- You must come to recognize and accept that God is wholly harmless, wholly benign, wholly loving, or you will be unable to strengthen your connection to Him. Instead, you will continue to avoid Him and prolong your stay from home.

Radiant Meditation:

From lesson 189 in the Workbook   **ACIM-W.359**

Sit in silence with your eyes shut for at least a minute saying these words in your mind:

I feel the love of God within me now.

Awaken Your Consciousness

A C T I V I T Y   # 1

Imagine for a moment what it would feel like to be completely without fear or anxiety of any kind. There is no tension
in your body. No craving or lusting for people, substances, or
things. No disturbance in your mind. No anger, no guilt, no frus-
tration, no disappointment. There is no need to plan for a way
to make your life better. No feeling that you have to perform or
put out to be wanted, needed, or accepted. For one miraculous
instant, you realize the world is fine just the way it is, and you
are fine the way you are. You are completely at peace, and this
exquisite state is a first small inkling of what it feels like to be
open to receiving God's infinite love.

You are love

Love, which created me,
is what I am.   **ACIM-W.406**

*If you choose to see yourself as unloving,
you will not be happy.*   **ACIM-T.176**

*W*e are of God and are made in God's image. Therefore, what's true and real about us is wholly loving,
completely benign, and exquisitely perfect. Like God, what's
real about us wants to extend love. It wants love to go out
in all directions without any restriction. But unlike God,
we constrict love and hold it back because we have made
judgments about the worthiness of some beings. This withholding of love does not feel good. It hurts to constrict the
free flow of love. Literally, it hurts. How would it feel, for
example, if you had to hold an abdominal crunch for your
entire life? Could you do it? Could you do it and be happy?
Yet this is similar to the contracted pose that we routinely

hold for 75 or 85 years at a time. The holding back of love is an unnatural expression and is contrary to our nature.

All pain and suffering comes from our decisions to withhold our love and from our own belief that we are not wholly loving, completely benign beings. This unnatural constriction of love is the underlying cause of all addictions, all emotional pain, all physical pain, all sickness. It is the source of all fear, all anxiety, all worry. It is the cause of all feelings of emptiness. It is the reason why we are afraid to look within and see ourselves.

It is not possible to like ourselves if we do not recognize ourselves as loving beings. While it is very enjoyable and pleasant to receive love from others, this is not the way you recognize yourself as love. The recognition of self comes from being love, from demonstrating love, from extending love under challenging conditions. This is where the rubber hits the road, and this is where and how you learn who you are. It's easy to be loving when people and circumstances are agreeable, but it takes great intention and awareness to be loving when they're not. This awareness and intention is what you're after. Real, unshakeable self-esteem comes from the certain knowledge that we are love. Everything else is just window dressing.

But how can we simply be love? What does that really mean? It's confusing because love is an extremely broad term, and it means many, many different things to different people. If you take a poll of 20 people, you'll come up with 20 different definitions of love. If you read books about love, you will not get consistent direction about what it means to be a loving being. There's romantic love, puppy love, unrequited love, patriotic love, altruistic love, love of family, love of food. Some people believe that love is caring for another, or that it's being supportive, or showing affection, or being grateful. Other people may think that love requires sacrifice or loss of self. The point is not that any of these definitions are bad or wrong. Rather, it's to underscore how ambiguous it is to figure out what it means to be a loving being. For example, if you're not a particularly affectionate person, does that then mean you're not a loving person?

To find common ground, it's useful to think about love in terms of the lowest denominator that everyone can agree on. And here it is. Love is always harmless. Or said another way, **love is not attack.** This one seemingly simple realization will enable you to navigate through every kind of challenging situation in a safe, powerful, and magnificent way. If we consistently make the decision to do the harmless thing, then we will begin to recognize ourselves as loving beings. Harmlessness enables us to like ourselves and others. Harmlessness enables us to feel good about ourselves and others. When we become harmless, we do not scare ourselves with our own behavior. We do not have anything to hide. We do not have anything to take from others. It is the foundation for our happiness.

Our true, eternal self offers love that is harmless, free (without obligation of any kind), and non-specific to all beings. Our individual and collective mission is to remove the blocks that prevent us from recognizing ourselves as this radiant, blazing, impersonal love. There's nothing else to do. We're already perfect. There's only stuff to undo. We have to get everything out of the way that prevents us from seeing our own loving perfection. We begin the process of undoing through the conscious practice of harmlessness. Let it infiltrate your life.

First, we become aware of the truth, that we are love. Then we begin to occasionally live this truth. We *are* love, consciously and intentionally, at least some of the time. Then we are love more frequently because we discover that it's the only thing that makes us happy. And then, one day, we are only love, only harmless. This is how our personal transformation will come about. It is a quiet, subtle, but dramatic process that impacts every aspect of our lives.

Why is it critically important to recognize that we are love?

- The expression of love is the only thing that's real about us. Everything that comes through us that is not love is false and unreal.

- Every time we make the decision to withhold love, we are repeating our decision to be unlike God, to separate from Him, and to keep ourselves out of heaven.

- Every time we make the decision to withhold love, we are making a choice to hurt ourselves and to be unhappy. The decision to withhold love is the cause, and suffering is the effect.

💗 The deliberate and conscious choice to refrain from attack and to be love is the answer to every problem.

Radiant Meditation:

From lesson 170 in the Workbook   **ACIM-W.326**

Sit in silence with your eyes shut for at least a minute saying these words in your mind:

There is no cruelty in God and none in me.

Awaken Your Consciousness

A C T I V I T Y   # 2

Instead of picturing yourself as needy or desperate for love, you now have a beginning awareness of yourself as the source of love. You realize that the world is starving for love, and you provide it. Your love is freely given to anyone. There are no conditions or expectations for anything in return. This giving of love is not experienced as strong desire, as an emotional attachment, or as a way to direct and control your life experience. Rather, it's a subtle sensation of energy going out from your body. Something invisible extends out from you. With each out-breath, you notice a subtle feeling. The feeling is strongest at the crown area of your head, but you can feel energy moving out of you from every surface inch of skin. Try, now, to notice and hold this exquisite sensation for the next 30 seconds.

The frequent practice of giving love leaves you feeling energized, alive, and vital. Try this exercise whenever you feel drained or depressed. It will uplift you.

God is formless

To be without a body is to be in our natural state. **ACIM-W.125**

I am not a body. I am free. For I am still as God created me. **ACIM-W.386**

You cannot enter into real relationships with any of God's Sons unless you love them all and equally. Love is not special. **ACIM-T.265**

A basic understanding of the difference between form and formlessness is critically important to make logical, informed decisions about your belief system. We know that God is formless because God is completely invisible to our human senses. Look around. Do you see God? Do you hear God? Can you touch Him? Taste Him? Smell Him? No, you only recognize God indirectly through life forms. There's nothing you can point to and say, "Aha, there he is!" We can only discern God's presence. For example, there's a very discernable difference between a human corpse, which is only physical form, and an alive human being, which is physical form plus God's mysterious Life-force energy. If you took a living human body and cut it open to study it, you would not be able to identify the condition or thing that makes it alive or divine. You could see the signs of life—the heart beating, breath coming through the mouth or nose, movements of all kinds—but you could not see the Life-force itself. And this is how we know, without any doubt or hesitation, that God is completely invisible and formless. Our belief in this mysterious formlessness is demonstration of faith.

Form, on the other hand, requires no faith whatsoever. Who doubts our earthly world of humans, animals, plants, mountains, buildings, and things? *Seeing is believing.* And seeing is enough for most people. Our money says *In God We Trust.* But to be more accurate, it should really say "in form we trust." We are more likely to believe in what we can perceive with our senses than we are to believe in what we can't see with our senses. Therefore, tangible form *seems* more real, and an intangible God *seems* more false, or at least questionable.

Faith is needed to believe there's another world. This formless world is heaven, and it is God's realm. Everything in God's world is formless. Peace is formless. Joy is formless. Love is formless. Power is formless. There are no malls in heaven. No neighborhoods. No parking lots. Since we are God's creations, it follows that what's real about us is also formless. Big Heart uses the Course term, *Christ,* as the name for our formless, divine self. Growth comes from the conscious willingness to recognize our Christ-self, to treat others with Christ-self awareness, and to rely on our Christ-self to prevent and/or correct mistakes.

Many people routinely deny any conscious awareness of their divine Christ-self. While this lack of awareness does not negate the power in any way, it does dramatically inhibit its expression. This also greatly diminishes enjoyment of life and creates confusion about life purpose. Anger, guilt, unhappiness, and feelings of low self-esteem come from the mistaken belief that we are limited, powerless, victims of circumstance. Inner peace, happiness, and other good feelings are an automatic by-product of rediscovering your own inherent formless self.

Despite this persuasive logic, form has great seduction and appeal. Form enables us to *think* we are separate from God and to be different and distinct from one another. Distinction is important because that's how we garner special attention for ourselves. As you already know, God created us formless, in his image. In His world we are equal and indistinct from one another. But we prefer form so that we can get the individual attention that we crave. Physical appearance, physical performance, gender, and racial differences enable us to be different and special. This is the heart of our darkness. We want to be special, and God's love is not special in any way.

What's real about us is not the form. It's what's inside the form. People who have physical

handicaps or great beauty often develop a keen
awareness that's what's real about them is not
what's seen by others. Ask Christopher Reeves,
and he'll tell you that this is true. He is still
himself even though his bodily form is not fully
functional. Women who have had mastectomies
and people who have had limbs amputated
acquire this awareness. What's real has not been
changed, threatened, or diminished by the condition of the bodily form around it.

Here on earth everyone believes they're one-of-a-kind,
never to be replaced or replicated. No two in the whole
wide world are quite the same. No one who came before
was ever the same. No one who comes in the future will be
the same either. We are taught and firmly believe that
everyone has something special and unique to offer the
world. We are universally encouraged to discover this specialness, and to develop, and express it. You may have heard
the phrase "nature abhors sameness." What we're really saying is that nature, or another code name for God, has mandated we be different from each other and that we celebrate
and exploit that difference. We all believe this is true and
never question it. Nature, of course, continually affirms and
demonstrates this point to us. No two fingerprints are
exactly alike. No two DNA prints are exactly alike. Not
even identical twins are exactly alike. Each snowflake is different. Each water drop is different. Each grain of sand is
different.

Of course, when we develop spiritual vision, we will come to *see* that no one is different. No thing that contains life is different. We are all exactly the same. All life is exactly the same.

Pretend you're on your deathbed with only 24 hours to live. Death forces you to cut to what's really important. Would you care about your bank account? Would you care about your body weight? Would you care about your career or social status? No, you would discover that all you really care about is your love in your heart for others, and their love for you. We do not have to wait until the end of our lives to come to the realization that form is not important.

Why is it critically important to recognize that God is formless?

- God is formless and our Christ-self is formless. What's real and eternal cannot be seen.

- Faith or spiritual vision is needed to consciously override what we perceive with our senses and to believe in the existence of Christ in ourselves and others.

- Even though love itself cannot be seen, the effects of love can be demonstrated and witnessed. We need to demonstrate to ourselves that we are loving beings. We need to witness our own love to believe it.

- Human love is typically specific, which means that love is given to selected people or things who meet certain criteria.

God's love is general, which means that love is given to everything, without regard to forms or conditions of any kind. Special love is unlike God's love.

- The quest for special attention distracts us from remembering that we are the love we seek.

Radiant Meditation

From lesson 94 in the Workbook   **ACIM-W.164**

Sit in silence with your eyes shut for at least a minute saying these words in your mind:

I am as God created me.

Awaken Your Consciousness

A C T I V I T Y   # 3

The light you seek is already within you. It is strong and pure and sure and kind. For one minute, or for as long as you feel comfortable, bring your Christ-self to your consciousness. Sit comfortably in silence. When you're ready, shut your eyes. Clear your mind of any disruptive thoughts and fill it with a picture of the most radiant, shimmery, glistening light. Let the light fill your body. Concentrate on the sensation of heightened awareness that this exercise produces.

We made the world

The world as you perceive it cannot have been created by the Father, for the world is not as you see it. God created only the eternal, and everything you see is perishable. Therefore, there must be another world that you do not see. **ACIM-T.210**

The Holy Spirit is not concerned with form, being aware only of meaning. **ACIM-T.162**

raditional Judeo-Christian theology teaches that God expelled us from the Garden of Eden (where life was perfect) because we were disobedient, wayward children who did something bad we weren't supposed to do. The basic idea is that God put us here as a kind of time out place for our punishment. Many of us believe we are here to experience pain and suffering until we come to our senses, confess or atone for our badness, and die. We are also taught that at the moment of our death God will judge us and our earthly performance. If our performance is good enough, we will be allowed to reunite with Him and with the other do-gooders in heaven, where we will experience eternal love and life. And if we're not good enough, we will be doomed to a life of eternal banishment, pain, and suffering in hell along with the other hell-raisers.

An updated interpretation, using *A Course In Miracles*® as a reference point, teaches that we are not conscious of being with God, in this moment, because we do not choose to be conscious of Him. *We made our world of form so that we can pretend to be separate from God, and to forget Him as much as humanly possible.* God hasn't thrown us out of His world. We've thrown ourselves out. God has not judged us as unworthy. We've chosen to leave Him and to experience life in a way that is unlike Him. We're here by choice. That's the bottom line. And this decision will stay in effect, until we change our minds and consciously make another decision.

We *want* to be here. Our families are here. Our friends are here, our houses, our jobs. Who wants to be without them? Our bank accounts, our TVs, our malls, our natural wonders, and our endless pursuit of entertainment are here. Who can live without these excitements and distractions? For most of us, the prospect of not being here on earth is deeply disturbing and extremely unappealing. We do not want to experience life in any other way. And so we actively resist the idea that any other way of life is possible. Even our vision of heaven is a kind of earth-like experience, only better.

Since we are totally hooked on our earthly experience, we do not recognize form as a limit. It follows, then, that we are equally unconscious of the rules about form that "program," "govern," and dramatically stop more creative thinking. There are four key so-called rules about form to reconsider:

1. **Form makes you safe.**
    Feelings of security, privilege, comfort, and pleasure are directly linked to form. The form that is most appealing and that makes us feel the most secure or insecure is our body. Think about all the attention you pay to your body—appearance, health, functionality, physical worthiness and acceptability.

    Form can also be less obvious. For example, there is form in habits, rituals, and routines. We like to do things that we don't have to think about doing and that are "tried and true." Repetitive behavior patterns give us a false sense of security.

2. **The accumulation of form is power.**
    The more form you have, the more you think you are entitled to special attention. Therefore, the acquisition of form is a major life activity and distraction. Success is measured and displayed through form. We all know the drill. More money is better. A bigger house is better. A higher degree is better. A more expensive car is better. A job with more prestige is better. Being married has more prestige than being single. Marriage is the joining of two forms. Being part of a family has more prestige than just being a couple. A family is the joining of

three or more forms. People who have more friends are perceived as more successful than people who have few friends. And so on.

3. **Perfect form is better and more valuable**
We are particularly fond of forms that are perfect, large, rare, natural, beautiful, expensive, pure, or clean. These are all earthly qualities that are universally sought and valued. For example, the rarer the form, the higher the value. Or the bigger the form, the greater the value. This applies to natural phenomena, people, money, collections. Common forms and imperfect forms are judged as less worthy.

4. **Form has intelligence**
The decision to make form came from our minds. This gives mind dominion over physical form. The idea of "mind over matter" is not new, yet most of us do not really believe that we have this amazing power. We prefer to think we are powerless victims of circumstance, but we are not. Decisions that impact our bodies and our world are constantly and routinely made, but we are unaware of them. This lack of awareness does not negate the power in any way.

Examine your own belief system now and consider whether you are denying your power. Do you endow your body with inherent intelligence? For example, we frequently hear about the "wisdom of the body" or the idea that "the body knows best." But the body is just form and does not contain intelligence. Intelligence only comes from the mind. Every cell is a willing slave in service to decisions and desires made in the mind. If you make the decision to feel bad about yourself, then your body will likewise follow suit. The body is an accurate reflection of every thought or feeling that we have. This makes the body an excellent device for increasing awareness of unconscious decisions because it is extremely difficult to deny a bodily malfunction. If the malfunction is severe enough, it literally forces you to reexamine your thoughts and behaviors.

Thoughts, feelings, and behaviors are also under control of the mind. Although we don't usually bother to do it, we can choose which thoughts and feelings to keep and which ones to toss. The realization that thoughts of light or darkness in our own minds can influence our physical condition is the basis for healing and miracle work. Thoughts of light or love heal the body, and thoughts that do not display love have the potential to harm the body. It's as simple and mysterious as that.

Earthly form is not made from love. It's made from the decision to separate from love. This doesn't mean that form is bad or that it should be treated in a loveless, absent-minded, or rejecting way. It doesn't mean that we should pretend it doesn't exist, either. Form is part of our earthly experience and takes on whatever meaning we give it. It becomes a useful tool towards spiritual awakening when we use the earth, our relationships, and our things to demonstrate and communicate our intention to be holy and harmless. It is not possible to be completely harmless and support our own life form, but we can at least be as harmless as humanly possible. The decision to be harmless leads to the irrelevance of form because then form has no influence on your behavior. It doesn't matter whether we're making decisions concerning the earth, concerning our bodies, or other life forms. We can choose to be harmless and to extend our love to all.

Why is it critically important to recognize that we make the world?

- We have used our power to make the physical world that we live in and to live in this realm. Therefore, we likewise have the power to unmake the world, or to choose to live in a heavenly realm.

- Form and conventional ideas we have about form are limitations. "The very nature of true perception is that it has no limits. It is the opposite of the way you see now." **ACIM-W.1**

- The decision to become harmless leads to the irrelevance of form because the decision to be harmless is general and applies to all conditions and situations.

Form is completely controlled by the mind. With the help of the Holy Spirit, we have the power to change form, to perform miracles, and to heal ourselves and others.

Radiant Meditation:

From lesson 32 in the Workbook **ACIM-W.49**

Sit in silence with your eyes shut for at least a minute saying these words in your mind:

I have invented the world I see.

Awaken Your Consciousness

ACTIVITY #4

(Adapted from lesson 1 in the Workbook)
The purpose of this exercise is to begin the radical realization that our earthly experience does not come from God. It comes from us. We choose the experience. Therefore, the meanings we assign to worldly things and experiences do not come from God. They come from us. These earthly ideas are conventions that we all buy into and agree on. We are attached to them.

For the next minute or two, you are asked to gently loosen your attachment and think in an unconventional way. Casually look at the objects in the room you're sitting in. Let your eyes move indiscriminately from one thing to another without attaching any particular importance or significance to any object. Don't intentionally exclude or include anything. As you identify each thing, say to yourself, "This _____ does not mean anything."

> Example:
> This door does not mean anything.
> This chair does not mean anything.
> This table does not mean anything.
> This carpet does not mean anything.

This is a simple but difficult exercise. It's simple because anyone can look around a room and identify objects. But it's difficult because we really don't want to tamper with our core beliefs about the world. Resist the urge to skip over the exercise. At the very least, introduce this new idea into your mind and "try it on for size". You don't have to keep the idea. Just be aware that another perception of the world exists.

RADIANT IDEA 5

Life is but a dream

The choice is not between which dreams
to keep, but only if you want to live in dreams
or to awaken from them.   **ACIM-T.612**

Yet the Bible says that a deep sleep fell
upon Adam, and nowhere is there reference
to his waking up.   **ACIM-T.18**

Dreams are perceptual temper tantrums, in which
you literally scream, "I want it thus!"   **ACIM-T.376**

ur experience of life is the dream or the illusion that we can be separate from God. Of course, in reality, we cannot be separate from our Source. We can temporarily give ourselves amnesia and forget God. We can distract ourselves into thinking He is not there. We can fool ourselves into thinking that God is to be feared and should therefore be avoided. We can trick ourselves into thinking that we are weak, needy, frail, sick, and vulnerable. We can do all these things, but we cannot undo the inherent, changeless, eternal link that connects God to us and to each other. It is immutable.

Our entire life is spent dreaming. We have sleeping dreams, and we have awake dreams. It's easy to acknowledge our sleeping dreams. These dreams seem vivid and real and full of emotion while they're happening. But then, as our eyes open to the morning, we realize we were sleeping, and nothing really happened to us. There actually is nothing under the bed or in the closet that's going to get us. However, it requires more effort and willingness to recognize our *awake dreams.*

Awake dreams are also vivid and emotionally-charged, but they're more subtle. Our awake dreams are in the form of grudges, expectations, fantasies, worries, and plans. We all hold a vision of how life *should be* or of how life *should have been.* As of the year 2000, there are over six billion people on earth. That means there are over six billion visions of how life *should be.* And there are over six billion nightmares of how poorly or unjustly we've been treated in the past. Therefore, our attention is not on what is. It's on what was or what may be. We dream whenever we reject the present moment and live in the future or the past.

> I have personally spent much of my life rushing through the present moment to get to the next one. I rush through my household chores so I can get to work. I rush through my work so I can take some free time for myself. I rush through

my free time for myself so I can get home and be with family. I rush through my family time so I can finally get some rest. I worry through my rest time about all there's left to do. This is not living! This is the dream of living, and it is not enjoyable.

Note that our attention is the indicator of what we want. If we want the present moment, we want life. If we don't want the present moment, we want the dream of life. We all reject the present moment in favor of something that really doesn't exist. We are routinely taught and coached to choose the dream of life over the actual experience of life. Dream big, they say. Live your dreams. Success, we're told, is the ability to make a big, beautiful dream and then achieve it. Yet while goals and dreams may be delightful, they can also get in the way of enjoying the present. For example . . .

- The dream of finding the perfect life partner gets in the way of experiencing what your present partner has to offer, or of being a great partner because you do not fit someone else's dream criteria.
- The dream of having perfect parents gets in the way of experiencing the best aspects of your real parents, or of being a loving parent because you don't match a child's dream image.
- The dream of bringing up the perfect child gets in the way of fully experiencing the raising of your actual

children, or of being a wonderful child because you are criticized for having your own unique dream.

In our fantasies, everyone does what we want them to do. In these dreams, things turn out the way *we* want them to turn out. Since we're the director of the show, we call the shots. Well, the reality is that the players in our dream might have their own ideas about how the drama should turn out. It's highly likely that they'll do what they want to do instead of what we wish. So we get upset, hurt, disappointed, disillusioned, and/or turned off.

Scratch beneath the surface of every feeling of anger, and you'll quickly see your reaction is due to someone not fulfilling the dream role you assigned to them. A person didn't behave the way that you, master of the dream universe, wanted them to behave. He or she didn't say the words that you wanted them to say. He or she didn't express the feelings that you wanted them to demonstrate. So you get angry! In a way, dreams are a kind of protest against reality. You are protesting about people being the way they are, instead of the way you want them to be. This can make life quite hard, and it's how the dream of life works against you.

Why is it critically important to realize we are dreaming?

🩶 Expectations, grudges, fantasies, worries, and plans are all a form of awake dreaming.

🍬 People don't disappoint us. Only our dreams of what people are *supposed* to do can let us down. Still, each disappointment can be a wake-up call to simply stop dreaming.

🍬 *The only way to stop dreaming is pay attention to what is, the present moment.*

Radiant Meditation:

From lesson 194 in the Workbook   **ACIM-W.370**

Sit in silence with your eyes shut for at least a minute saying these words in your mind:

I place the future in the Hands of God.

Awaken Your Consciousness

A C T I V I T Y # 5 :

Your mission is to make your life count *now*, instead of dreaming about how it will count when conditions are more acceptable, or more perfect. Do this by paying full attention to each activity that makes up your day. Start with the realization that everything you do is of equal importance. So, for example, washing dishes is no less important than whatever it is you do to earn money.

The act of washing dishes is made important by putting your full attention on it. For if you do this chore in a mindless, distracted way, you reject the moment in favor of the next activity. The next thing is, of course, perceived as either more important or more enjoyable. In essence, rushing through dishwashing is like saying this moment of your life isn't important and doesn't really count so you don't have to pay attention to it.

Most of our activities are done in a habitual, routine way. The internal robot takes over. As a result, our days end up being a collection of moments that don't count. And our lives end up being a collection of days that don't count. Then, of course, the perfect moment never arrives. The perfect people never manifest. So life is never really lived.

As an alternative, try this experiment in living. For one half-hour, pay full attention to everything you do. Make yourself happy by bringing quality to each act. Think about how you can uplift an activity so that it's the highest and best experience that it can possibly be. Bring this intention and conscious awareness to the most mundane tasks: driving a car, going to an ATM machine, or doing the laundry. If your mind starts to plan, worry, or wander, just gently bring it back to what you're doing. This is how you begin to imbue your life with meaning and purpose.

The ego is the dreamer

Everyone makes an ego or a self for himself,
which is subject to enormous variation
because of its instability. **ACIM-T.56**

You made the ego without love, and so
it does not love you. **ACIM-T.100**

The concept of the self has always been
the great preoccupation of the world.
And everyone believes that he must find the
answer to the riddle of himself. **ACIM-T.659**

he ego is a sophisticated term, which is used to describe the collection of ideas each of us has about our "self." Everyone makes an ego for himself or herself. It perceives itself as the center of its universe. *For the ego, everything revolves around me, me, me. My* opinions are valuable. *My* feelings are important. *My* family is best. *My* job is relevant. *My* wishes are to be respected. *My* values are the standard by which life should be lived. *My* ideas are the most worthy ones. *My* sickness is the worst. *My* children are the most delightful. *My* problems are the most upsetting. *My* religion is the only true path. And on and on. The ego is the source of the belief that we can forget our Creator, take His Life-force and power, and independently make ourselves and our world without Him. This dreamer of the dream against life, the ego, has also been known as the anti-Christ, the devil, or Satan!

The challenge is that the ego and our Christ-self both share the mind. We get thoughts from the ego through our mind, and we get thoughts from our Christ-self from there as well. This is what the Course means when it says our mind is split. The mind, however, is like a radio and can only hear one station at a time. The ego station is very noisy, dramatic, and entertaining. The Christ-self station can only be heard when the mind is still and at peace. The ego-self shouts; the Christ-self whispers. *Most of us only listen to our ego and rarely, if ever, intentionally tune in to our Christ-self.* In fact, the ego does everything it possibly can to minimize our will-ingness to put the mind at peace. It demands constant busy-ness, constant attention, constant distraction. Who wants to sit in peace, quiet, and stillness when there are more interest-ing and sensational things to do?

We know that our Christ-self comes from God because it never changes. It cannot be undone. It cannot be made more perfect. While it's possible to forget or ignore our

Christ-self, it is not possible to undo it. Our Christ-self is immutable.

The ego, on the other hand, is subject to enormous volatility. As you know, thoughts, moods, and feelings can swing or change in an instant. In fact, the ego depends on certain conditions for its stability and happiness and reacts whenever specifications are not met. Since the nature of our earthly world is conditional, the ego is constantly reacting and striving. We know that the ego does not come from God because of this changeable quality. We also know that the ego does not come from God because it can be temporarily overridden and even completely undone. Whenever the mind is at peace, the ego is overridden and the Christ-self shines through.

The idea of undoing the ego can be a very scary notion. The prospect of losing the thoughts we call *me* or *self* produces extreme fear and resistance. The ego does not want to be undone and will actively work against these efforts. If the ego's sense of security, comfort, control, or happiness is threatened in any way, it immediately resorts to harmfulness. For example, whenever the ego is threatened or frightened, it will always counsel you to think, talk, or act in ways that result in attack, separation, or suspicion.

The myth of the vampire is actually a description of the ego:

- The vampire lives in the dark. The ego lives in the dark.
- The vampire believes that light will harm it. The ego thinks that light will harm it.

- The vampire stays alive by attacking other humans. The ego stays alive by attacking other humans.
- The vampire is afraid of God. The ego is afraid of God.
- The vampire is undone by a silver bullet or a stake through the heart. A silver bullet and a stake through the heart are metaphors for truth. The ego is also undone by truth.

We are taught that we need a strong ego to survive, to get what we want from life, and to be happy. People with quiet egos are perceived as weak or as doormats for others. They are deemed to be undesirable role models for a successful life. Much emphasis is placed on having high self-esteem. From the ego's perspective, self-esteem is a collection and measure of external indicators of worthiness. This includes respect received from others, recognition of our accomplishments from others, having our feelings validated by others, love and special attention received from others, support received from others, sympathy received from others, and so on. In fact, the ego constantly compares and measures its value and worth by the amount of attention it gets from others.

Any attention, even so-called bad attention, can be desirable. Therefore, the ego is constantly in the act of hooking attention for itself. This constant seeking of attention makes us needy and vulnerable. We routinely use the giving of attention and/or the withdrawal of attention to hook and control other egos. One ego will capriciously withdraw attention or love whenever another ego does not live up to his or her dream role. Or it will lavish attention to ensure commitment and loyalty. We spend most of our lives trapping or being trapped by the attention we get or don't get from other egos. It is a huge distraction! When we're focused on giving or getting ego attention, we're not conscious of our Christ-self or thinking about God.

Our Christ-self recognizes that we are like God and are therefore already all powerful. The ego, on the other hand, sees itself as weak and needing something outside itself to solve problems and make itself happy. Here are some of the typical things the ego seeks to be happy:

- If only I had more money, then I'd be happy.
- If only I had a new car, then I'd be happy.
- If only my breasts (or penis) were bigger, then I'd be happy.
- If only I weighed less, then I'd be happy.
- If only I had better medicine, then I'd be happy.
- If only the stars were aligned to support my sign, then I'd be happy.
- If only I had a more loving partner in life, then I'd be happy.
- If only I had a job that I liked, then I'd be happy.
- If only the world and the people in it were perfect, then I'd be happy.

Unfortunately, there is no end to the allure of things. Once the ego gets the desired object, it's still unhappy because the next dream is now on the radar screen. So it wants the next thing or the next person. And then, the next, and the next, and the next, and the next. It never ends! We live our lives with a big hole in our hearts, always lusting for or dreading the next thing on the never-ending "to do list."

The only reprieve from this constant hunger or dread is to tune out the ego and listen to your other station. It offers Christ-self programs, 24 hours a day, seven days a week. The Christ-self that abides within calls us away from misery and towards happiness. He will not ask us to sacrifice our desires. He will only ask us to see them from another perspective.

The Course provides us with two powerful and surprisingly simple tools for turning out the ego. One tool is the *holy instant of peace* and the other is *forgiveness.*

- The first tool, the holy instant of peace, is a moment of stillness in which we're not thinking or doing anything. It's important to note that we don't have to be holy to utilize this gentle tool. Rather, we become holy by using the holy instant. Holiness happens whenever we consciously override the impulse to hate or to be harmful with the decision to be harmless. A moment of stillness enables us to tune into our Christ-self and neutralize any harmful thoughts. Then our Christ-self can help us to harmlessly decide what to do, if anything, about the provocation of the moment. The holy instant enables us to tap into His strength, His wisdom, His plan, His love.
- The second technique for tuning out the ego is forgiveness. As you can imagine, the ego's definition of

forgiveness is different than the Holy Spirit's definition of forgiveness. The ego wants to assign blame. It
wants to give or get apologies. It wants justice. Justice,
or retribution, is really the socially-condoned return of
hate for hate. This version of forgiveness does not end
hate. Instead, it extends it. Real forgiveness is harmless
because it stops the otherwise endless chain of hate.
Where will hate end if not with you? The only thing
the Holy Spirit wants is to erase the hateful thoughts
from your mind. All that's required to do this is a
change of mind. We used to think that we or someone
else was bad or wrong, and now we don't. That's all
there is to it.

The ego can be tuned out, but we have to *want* to tune it
out. It came into your mind through invitation and leaves
when the invitation is withdrawn. When you create a
peaceful, non-judgmental state of mind, the ego gets bored
and wants to leave. There's no struggle, no resistance, no
hate. Just stillness.

Why is this idea critically important?

- The ego is fickle and constantly changing. Your Christ-self
  is stable and changeless.

- The ego is not our friend and cannot be trusted to lead us
  to happiness because it will always resort to attack to get
  what it wants.

- The ego is very tricky. It cannot be disengaged or transcended through struggle, control, punishment, or harshness. Therefore, it is useless to hate or reject the ego. This is counterproductive because it keeps the ego strong and intact. Rather, accept the ego, and make the harmless choice to override it through inner peace and forgiveness.

- The ego must be disengaged to recognize and hear the Christ-self within.

- We can temporarily and even permanently live without an ego.

Radiant Meditation:

From lesson 309 in the Workbook   **ACIM-W.454**

Sit in silence with your eyes shut for at least a minute saying these words in your mind:

I will not fear to look within today.

Awaken Your Consciousness

A C T I V I T Y   # 6

Your mind is either asleep or it is awake. You can tell when it is sleeping because you will be thinking, talking, and acting in ways that are unlike God. You will see yourself as weak, needy, and/or hurt. You will see others as mean and vengeful. Your ego wants your mind to focus on fearful thoughts and to stay asleep because once your Christ-mind awakens, you will not want or need an ego anymore. Once your Christ-mind is awakened, you will rediscover that life can be lived without any mis-creative thoughts or actions.

Begin the joyful process of overriding your ego and rediscovering the glory that is your birthright. Do this by introducing new and uplifting thoughts into your mind. Transcend the constant fearful stream of thoughts that come from the ego with thoughts that lead you to change your mind. This change to a Christ-mind will enable you to recognize the truth about yourself and others. Say these words to yourself:

I am not weak, but strong.
I am not helpless, but all powerful.
I am not limited, but unlimited.
I am not doubtful, but certain.
I am not an illusion, but a reality.
I cannot see in darkness, but in light.   *ACIM.W.157*

Even just a moment of thought devoted to a change of mind will bring you closer to the rediscovery of light within yourself. Turn to these radiant and inspiring ideas whenever you need them.

Every decision is an act of power

*The power of decision is your only remaining
freedom as a prisoner of this world.* **ACIM-T.231**

*It is essential that error be not confused
with sin, and it is this distinction that makes
salvation possible.* **ACIM-T.402**

*The Son of God can be mistaken;
he can deceive himself; he can even turn
the power of his mind against himself.
But he cannot* sin. **ACIM-T.402**

*very decision is an act of power because every decision
has a consequence. The decision is the cause, and the
result of that decision is the consequence. This makes our decisions
extremely important.* We shape our experience in life
through our choices. In fact, every single thing that happens

to us is a direct result of our own decisions. Most decisions, however, are made in a reactionary, whimsical, or robotic way, where no awareness or deliberate thought goes into making the choice. For example, a response to provocation is usually done in an unconscious, tit-for-tat manner. Mindlessness is further compounded when awareness is clouded by the stupor of alcohol, drugs, excess food, or sexual lust. It is impossible to act or live with power when you don't know what you want, what you're doing, or why you're doing it. Hell is living with the consequence of one of our own undeliberated decisions.

Here are some decisions that produce results we don't really want:

- We make decisions to hate ourselves and each other.
- We make decisions to punish ourselves and each other.
- We make decisions to reject ourselves and each other.
- We make decisions to sacrifice our own happiness.
- We make decisions to spend our lives in front of the TV or computer.
- We make decisions to eat, drink, or drug when we would really rather not engage in these behaviors.
- We make decisions to do what society and other people think we "should" do instead of following our own hearts.

If your life experience is making you unhappy, then you must consider making another decision about how to live. Unhappiness comes from making decisions that are not working for you.

Problems are solved by paying attention to what you're doing and by fully experiencing the results. However, most of us mask or flee from feelings of unhappiness so quickly that we never develop awareness of how to stop being unhappy.

Some people need the intensity and inspiration of an extreme situation to bring a habitually flawed decision to their conscious attention. These crisis-type situations are perceived as unfortunate events. The Tibetans, however, have a more uplifting perspective. They say we should never judge an experience because we never know when we're having good luck! Events that force us to develop awareness of what we're doing are always beneficial even though they may temporarily feel uncomfortable. Discomfort is useful because it inspires us to pay attention to what we're doing and to stop making decisions that produce results we don't want. Correction is not possible if we're unaware of what we're doing, or if we're in denial. Once correction has been achieved, it's not necessary to hang on to uncomfortable feelings. Be a happy learner, and forgive yourself immediately for decisions made in the past that were mistakes!

Witnessing others make mistakes is another experience that is not typically perceived as good. Parents, children, spouses, friends, co-workers, and others who allow us to witness their big mistakes actually do us a great service. Through them, we can observe the consequences of decisions without having to figure it out through our own trial-and-error experience.

Decisions that are harmful to yourself, to others, or to any life form are mistakes. Our social system has a hierarchy for judging the okayness or badness of mistakes based on degree of harshness. For example, most people believe that thoughts are private, so therefore hateful thoughts are okay. The exchange of hateful words is not liked, but is usually tolerated. Hateful acts, however, are almost always punished. Acts that cause permanent damage are perceived as more serious than acts that cause temporary damage. And so on.

The problem is that the rules of our legal system and the morals of our social system are not in sync with God's plan for salvation. You are either harmful or harmless. You either make a mistake or you don't. There is no "in between" position. A mistake is not a sin; it's just a mistake. Sin is an ego concept to keep you fearful, emotionally upset, and distracted from seeing yourself in an untainted and holy way.

According to the ego, sin is eternal and can never be undone. It's a mark that stays with you forever. The presence of sin results in guilt, which requires punishment, suffering, and ultimately death. Mistakes, on the other hand, are decisions that need to be corrected. Of course, the baseline mistake that needs to be corrected is the decision to separate from God. *The correction of a mistake is not punishment. It's becoming aware that we can make another decision and then making it.*

We have the complete freedom and the power to experiment with the laws of cause and effect in any way. God does not usurp our power. He doesn't intervene and make decisions on our behalf. Nor does he undo the consequences of decisions that we have made. This is interference, and interference would be a limitation on our power. The Holy Spirit, however, has the role of using every situation for good.

We also have the power to use every situation for good. Goodness is getting what you want in a way that does not hurt yourself or anyone else. What is it you want? Do you know? *Take the time to always know your own Christ-mind before mindlessly deciding and acting.* This saves enormous amounts of otherwise wasted time and fills your acts with power.

The world is very tentative. Conditions are always changing. Nothing is for sure. Just when you think that you've got things under control, the rug slips out from under you. The only thing you have to hold on to are your own decisions. When your decisions are strong, unwavering, and firm, your life experience becomes strong, unwavering, and firm. It doesn't matter what's going on around you, so long as you hold firmly to your decision.

When your decisions are haphazard, chaotic, or whimsical, your life experience is confused and chaotic. Why? Because you're constantly changing your mind and revising your decisions based on what's happening around you instead of what you want. Routine, seemingly insignificant decisions are the ones that can be most difficult. Witness, for example, how hard it is to hold the decision to stop smoking, or to lose weight, or to stop swearing. *Can you begin to see how making mindful decisions and holding on to your own decisions will make a major difference in the quality of your life?*

Why is this idea critically important?

- A mistake is an unconscious decision to be harmful.

- All mistakes are repetitious forms of the decision to separate from God. The return to God and the undoing of mistakes are the same because they both require the decision to become harmless.

- God does not ask for punishment of decisions that are mistakes. He asks that we change our minds and make another choice. God waits in patience and without judgment for our change of mind.

- God does not intervene to undo our decisions because that would usurp and limit our power, but the Holy Spirit can make all things right and transmute all situations for healing and good.

Radiant Meditation:

From lesson 152 in the Workbook   **ACIM-W.281**

Sit in silence with your eyes shut for at least a minute saying these words in your mind:

The power of decision is my own.

Awaken Your Consciousness
ACTIVITY # 7

The decision that always prevents mistakes is the choice to be at peace. This doesn't mean that you shouldn't want other things or that you can't have them. Rather, it means that all worldly desires should be fulfilled in a peaceful way. The way of peace may not be the quickest way to get something, but it will allow you to experience happiness because it enables you to feel good about yourself and others *during* the process of living.

Whenever you decide to value something else the world offers more than you value peace, you will experience unhappiness. It's really as simple as that. Still, it takes considerable awareness and several, repetitive and sometimes painful experiences, to come to realize that your own non-peaceful decisions are the source of your own unhappiness. Perhaps, for example, you want to be adored by your spouse, but your spouse is not treating you in an adoring way. When you value adoration over peace, you feel justified in getting angry or attacking your spouse because you haven't gotten what you want. But when you value peace above all other things, you can do without adoration for the moment. The peaceful moment enables you to focus on what you want. Then you can consciously direct yourself to be more creative and get what you want without resorting to attack.

Getting what you want is really up to you. It requires thinking and then acting in a more creative way. In the above situation, perhaps you would have to wait for a time when your spouse is more mellow or open and then gently ask again. Or maybe you would have to be clearer about what adoration means to you. Or maybe you would have to demonstrate adoration in your own behavior. Or you might need to envision being adored in your mind. There are many other more creative courses of action that you can take without resorting to anger. When you make the choice for peace, you can figure them out. Your job is to keep trying until you come up with the solution that works.

In real life, most of us tend to focus on the problem instead of the solution. This is because the problem is a form, and it's very tangible. We see it, live with it, angst about it. The solution, however, is not so tangible. It exists only in your mind and requires faith to believe it will come about. Unfortunately, when you focus on the problem, then that's what you get more of. Do the hard thing and put your attention on what you want, not on what you don't want.

Think about a current problem in your life. What do you want? Envision the perfect solution in your mind. See it. Feel it. Believe it's possible. Now think of one small act that you and you alone can do differently to slowly move toward the solution you see in your mind.

God wills your happiness

You must ask what God's Will is in everything,
because it is yours. You do not know what it is, but
the Holy Spirit remembers it for you. Ask Him,
therefore, what God's Will is for you, and He will tell
you yours. It cannot be too often repeated that you
do not know it. **ACIM-T.196**

We have no will apart from His,
and all of us are one because His Will is
shared by all of us. **ACIM-W.466**

*M*any people are highly suspicious of doing God's Will. For one thing, it sounds very hokey and simple-minded, like something you'd read on a bumper sticker. But even more important, we may think that doing God's Will is contrary to our individual will. We might think He wants us to do something that we don't really want to do or wouldn't like doing. Maybe He wills us to change everything in our life as we know it and become selfless like a Mother Teresa. Or even worse, we could be afraid of God's Will. Maybe He wants us to sacrifice our children, like those stories contained in the Bible. Or maybe we think He wants to punish or destroy us, because we are so bad, so disobedient, and so wasteful. Truly, who would want to know or do God's Will if it's going to be so awful?

The most important thing to remember is that God is love and only love. He does not have an ego and is therefore not punitive, vengeful, demanding, or controlling. These are human ego characteristics, not divine ones. God is only good and therefore He wants only good for you. He wills your happiness. And why does he will your happiness? Because **your happiness is the one thing that makes you want to stay alive**. God is life, and He wills the experience that promotes and extends life.

When you ask to know God's Will, you are really asking to become aware of what makes you happy. As you repeatedly ask God for His Will over and over, you come to realize that He will lead you to happiness by always reminding you to extend your love. *Being* love is happiness now. It's a big leap in awareness to understand that *being* love is more useful and satisfying than getting a result or achieving a goal at some unknown future time. This is because form, no matter how pleasing or desirable, is a substitute for love, and will therefore not result in happiness. Things may pacify and distract you for a while, but they will not fill the empty hole in your heart.

There is a mistaken and deep-rooted belief that the will of the individual and the Will of God can be separate, but this is not possible. You want to be happy, and God wills you to be happy. So you see, the goal of happiness is the same. Your will to be happy cannot be separate or apart from His. So if your will and God's Will are the same, why bother to ask? This is a very appropriate question.

When you make decisions independently, without knowing God's Will, you are making a decision with your ego mind. As you already know, the ego is not your friend, and it will not advise you to think, talk, or act in ways that are always harmless. The reason for taking the time to ask God's Will is to disengage and filter out the ego. Then you can know, without any hesitation or doubt, which decisions will make you happy.

Many of us do not know how to make ourselves happy. Some of us think that our happiness is expendable or unimportant, so we willingly sacrifice it. However, the sacrifice of happiness does not lead to happiness. It leads to despair. Happiness is occasionally sacrificed as an offering to God, so that He will look down on us in mercy or favor. But our happiness is most frequently sacrificed in the name of maintaining a special relationship. Loss of self in another is not usually perceived as sacrifice. More typically, it takes on an elevated meaning. There are terms like "sacred love," or "holy matrimony." We all joyfully buy into the idea that a special relationship will make us happy and that getting and keeping a special relationship is the most important thing in our lives. This idea is based on the concept that we are incomplete and can be made complete by someone else. We think someone else can make us better than we are. Or that someone else can make us happy. Someone else wants you, so therefore you must be valuable, worthy, and lovable. This distracts you from doing the work of learning how to love yourself.

Authentic and real expression of self is often suppressed in the name of maintaining a special relationship. You don't say what you really think, because your partner, children, relatives, or friends won't like it or might get mad at you. You don't do what you really want to do, because they may disapprove or reject you. When you're authentic, you sometimes risk losing a relationship, experiencing anger from another, being shunned, and/or becoming the recipient of a variety of other unsavory treatments.

God wills us to make decisions that are loving to self as well as to others. By asking God's Will, we can always be sure that we are doing the right thing and that we're not forgetting our own happiness in the process. Asking first prevents mistakes, saves time, and fills our acts with boldness and confidence. When we're not timid, our acts become big and magnificent, because we are not withholding anything. A decision that is reached with the help of God becomes a full expression of being.

Even more, a decision that's in alignment with God's Will is a way of going with the Life-force, rather than against it. The characters in the Star Wars movie series would say, *May the Force be with you.* This is the little farewell prayer that the good guys say to each other before they start on a mission against the bad guys. It's their way of asking for life to win over death, or for light to overcome darkness. What we don't realize is that the Force is *always* with us. We, however, are not going with the Force when we give the ego control of our decisions.

In our fast-paced world, it's easy to forget to consider God's Will in every decision, but there is a way to remember. The reminder is your own misery! Whenever you're miserable, it's a sure sign that you have made an ego-based decision. This is the clue. Look for these clues in your life. Then ask to know God's Will in every situation, so that you can lift yourself up out of the muck and move yourself in a positive direction.

Why is the idea that God wills your happiness critically important?

- God is on your side. He will help you to find your way to happiness if you will let Him. God will not advise you to sacrifice yourself.

- You can't trust any decisions you make with your ego mind. Ask God's Will in every decision.

- Your happiness is directly linked to your will to stay alive. This makes your happiness very, very important.

Radiant Meditation:

From lesson 101 in the Workbook   **ACIM-W.182**

Sit in silence with your eyes shut for at least a minute saying these words in your mind:

God's Will for me is perfect happiness.

Awaken Your Consciousness

A C T I V I T Y   # 8

If you truly believe that God wills your happiness, then your personal happiness can and should be considered a great spiritual achievement. It's great because the world is basically an unhappy place. And it's an achievement, because happiness requires consistent effort. It comes from the deliberate, conscious choices you make concerning how you conserve or spend your life-energy. Deliberation and consciousness are the key words here.

Take the time now to deliberate about your own happiness. What are three or four things you like to do that make you happy? Don't just rush through this exercise to get it over with. Really think about it. What makes you happy? Now think about how to be more disciplined and passionate about bringing this happiness into your life on a regular basis. Can you do one thing each day that makes you happy? Will you do it?

We prefer that other people do the work of making us happy, but your personal happiness is your own responsibility. It takes a tiny bit of effort to become aware of your own requirements for happiness. And it takes a tiny bit more effort to act on that awareness. God wills you to be happy. You serve Him when you make your own happiness a top priority.

The answer to every problem is within

No force except your own will is strong enough or worthy enough to guide you. **ACIM-T.61**

Seek not outside yourself, for it will fail, and you will weep each time an idol falls. **ACIM-T.617**

The problem is not whether what the Holy Spirit says is true, but whether you want to listen to what He says. **ACIM-T.134**

We are trained to ask for advice, counsel, and answers from others. There's nothing wrong with asking for information and advice. In fact, it's often useful to gather information and opinions from others about issues that trouble us. Just keep in mind that you will not find egoless direction outside of yourself. Even the most well-intended, educated, intelligent people can be confused about what it means to be a loving and harmless being. Even the most well-intended, spiritual, or deeply religious people can lead you in a direction that is unproductive or in conflict with your authentic self. The earthly world is not about love, dear ones. It's about everything that blocks love. If it's your intention to be a more loving being, then you must go to an unworldly formless source for guidance.

Conveniently, you have that source inside you. It's your Christ-self. This is the Voice of the Holy Spirit, or the Universal Inner Teacher within. We can't all run off to Tibet or India to find a living egoless master to guide us. We don't have any swamis in our malls. But we all have an Inner Teacher. The challenge is to develop the willingness to tap into it. And then to trust that the message is real.

INNER TEACHER JOURNAL ENTRY: 04/04/2000

QUESTION: *Teacher, who are you? Are you me?*

ANSWER: I am not you, but I am you. I am the energy that connects. I am the connecting force. I am of the universe. I am available to all. That is who I am. I am of the mind and of the space around it. I am here to help you, to help you see, feel, and live the will of yourself and the Will of your Father. That is what I do. There is no need to worry about my intention. I am not mal-intended. I will not lead you astray. Only you can lead yourself astray. I will always point to the way of most use. That is what you most need to know about me.

Will you actually hear a voice? Well, perhaps. Some people do hear a voice. Some people have visions. Once in a great while, someone will have an extraordinary multi-sensory experience. But it's much more likely that the answer will come to you in an ordinary way. You'll get a very sure feeling, or a very definitive thought, or a set of very certain thoughts. And you will know, without any doubt, that it's the answer to your question.

Accessing your Inner Teacher is not hard, complicated, or involved. There's only one step, one thing to do. The ego needs to be temporarily disengaged through inner peace or stillness. This allows your Christ-self mind to shine through. As previously discussed, the mind is like a radio with two stations. When you still your mind, you click the ego station off and the Inner Teacher station on. A still mind is the only prerequisite. There are several techniques for achieving inner stillness and for communing with your Inner Teacher, but the simplest is to ask a question, quiet the mind, and wait for the answer.

The asking process is very easy. It's often also quick. Everyone can do it. No special skills are required. No special setting is needed. There's no need to push or strain for the answer. It may come right away. It may take several minutes. If you're tense or anxious about this process, the answer may come at a later time in an unguarded, relaxed moment, like when you're taking a shower or walking your dog. Just trust that if you ask the question, you will get an answer.

Your Inner Teacher will always direct you to think the highest thought of yourself or another. He will always direct you to make the most loving, harmless decision. He will not ask you to sacrifice yourself. He will help you to expand your perception and become big and magnanimous rather than small and petty. The more you rely on awareness of your Christ-self mind for decision-making, the happier you will be. Through your own trial-and-error experience, it eventually becomes obvious to you that ego-based decisions are not trustworthy, and in the long run, do not make you happy.

At first, you may only be inspired to go within for big decisions. As you become more familiar with the process, you'll realize that it takes very little effort to shift your awareness from your ego-mind to your Christ-self mind. The ultimate goal is to relinquish all independent decisions and to only make decisions with awareness of your Christ-self. This puts you in His service. This makes you His conduit.

Why is the idea that guidance comes from within critically important?

🍃 Your Inner Teacher, or Christ-self mind, is the only sure and reliable source for leading you to your happiness and for solving problems in a way that enables you to feel good about yourself and others.

🫘 The process of mining and extracting this love from inside yourself is the exquisite discovery that you are love. You are wise. You are big. You are everything you have ever wanted to be and more. The value of seeing your own worth is incomprehensible.

Radiant Meditation:

From lesson 303 in the Workbook   **ACIM-W.451**

Sit in silence with your eyes shut for at least a minute saying these words in your mind:

The holy Christ is born in me today.

Awaken Your Consciousness
A C T I V I T Y   # 9

The quickest route to happiness and conscious problem-solving is to ask for guidance from the Christ-self that dwells within. This Source of love is always there, always kind, always willing to help you to see your situation from the highest, most constructive perspective. There's only one trick. The voice for Christ can only be heard when your mind is at peace.

Find a place where you can sit in private without being disturbed. Allow yourself to just relax and to be still for a few moments. When you're ready, think of an issue in your life that's troubling you. Then phrase a question in your mind. Ask, "What do I need to know or do about _____ (the issue) to be happy?" Repeat the phrase three or four times until the question is firm in your mind. Then sit in peace and wait for the answer.

Hate has no meaning

*You will learn what you are from what you
have projected onto others.* **ACIM-T.114**

*The Holy Spirit does not want you
to understand conflict; He wants you
to realize that, because conflict is meaningless,
it is not understandable.* **ACIM-T.124**

*The logic of the world is totally insane
and leads to nothing.* **ACIM-T.271**

*A*s we have already discussed many times, God is only *love.* He has no awareness of anything that is not completely benign, harmless, and loving. In His world, there is no duality, no good and bad. There's only good. In fact, it's thought that the word "good" is a derivative of the word "God." In heaven there are no bad people and no bad experiences, there's only good. Therefore, in the real world, the formless world we do not see, hate does not exist and has no meaning.

This is completely different from our earthly experience. Here on earth, we not only like to see hate, we like to sensationalize it and draw as much attention to it as possible. One of the great preoccupations of the world is to point out hatefulness, especially in others. We love to talk about hate, study it, and analyze it. Our social, legal, and religious systems are set up to measure hate by degree of harm. We like to assign blame for hate. Our idea of justice is to receive payment or to inflict punishment for the hate that's been done to us. We are particularly fond of comparing our so-called *mild* forms of hatefulness to more dramatic expressions of hate, and judging ourselves as morally correct, righteous, and superior. We fool ourselves by thinking, "I am not so bad as you. I would never do anything as hateful as you." Whenever possible, we like to project our hate onto others. We are also particularly fond of repressing and denying our own hateful thoughts.

Why does hate exist? Why do hateful events happen in our world, or even to us personally? It's not possible for us to make sense out of the senseless. Since God did not create hate, it has no meaning. Even if we spend years analyzing and studying our own mistakes or the mistakes of others, all we will get for the exercise is a mind filled with false perceptions about hate. It's useful to remember that we get what we pay attention to. *All that we can know is that the Holy Spirit will use all situations for good. If we let Him, He will lift our perception to the highest level possible and enable us to view the situation through the eyes of kindness and love.*

The kindest interpretation is that hate is an expression of fear. Fear that we can't have what we want. Fear that we aren't worthy to have what we want. Fear that someone else might take something we want. Fear that our specialness is at risk. Here are three examples of False Evidence Appearing Real (FEAR) and how fear-based perception can be reinterpreted and raised by the Holy Spirit:

1. **EGO's senseless meaning:**
   My parent didn't love me, so that means I'm not worthy of love, and I'm not lovable. It also means I'm permanently damaged and will probably never be really loved by anyone.

   Holy Spirit's loving meaning:
   Perhaps it's the Holy Spirit's plan that you consciously use this situation to rediscover how to love yourself. Perhaps your parent did you a great service by providing you with the inspiration and opportunity to make this choice.

2. **EGO's senseless meaning:**
   My spouse left me, so that means my life is destroyed. I have lost everything that's familiar and important to me, and I may never recover. My life can only get worse.

   Holy Spirit's loving meaning:
   Perhaps the Holy Spirit's plan is for you to consciously use this situation to rediscover how to make

yourself happy. Perhaps your spouse did you a great service by providing you with the motivation to finally figure out how to make yourself a priority in your own life.

3. **EGO's senseless meaning:**
   My friend betrayed me, so that means I can never trust anyone. People easily forget all you've done for them, so why bother to even be kind or nice.

   Holy Spirit's loving meaning:
   Perhaps the Holy Spirit's plan is for you to consciously use this situation to overlook your friend's betrayal so that you can find the mercy within yourself to overlook your own mistakes towards others. Perhaps your friend did you a great service by demonstrating how really easy it is to overlook and forgive.

The bottom line is that we don't really know what <u>anything</u> means. We judge some conditions as bad and some others as good, but maybe the things that are called bad are really serving us in some extremely beneficial, mind-changing way. Still, it's very difficult to resist the inclination to assign meaning to hateful acts. Try to remember that this interpretation of events comes from our individual and collective egos, not from God. Our mistake is to trust our bodily senses rather than to trust the Christ in our self and in others. We think that what we see with our eyes is true, what we hear with our ears is true, and what we experience directly must be true. But hate is never true. The only thing that's true is the Christ-love that's blocked behind the hate. Therefore hate is not undone by the presence of more hate. It's only undone by removing the block to give or receive the expression of love.

As you've already read, there are two forms of hate. Anger is hate directed outward toward others, and guilt is hate directed inward toward the self. Some people think that one is worse than the other, but hate is hate. Both are equally destructive and senseless. When we see hate in ourselves, we hate ourselves for it. When we see hate in others, we hate them for it. The hardest thing you are asked to do is to see hate in yourself and others, and not automatically react to it. The response of hate to hate results in an endless chain of so-called *bad* karma. It's only *bad* because your meaningless act of retaliatory hate then becomes a cause that produces results you don't want. The hate you put out always comes back to you. And this is definitely *not* what you want!

The challenge is to accept rather than reject the hate. When you deny the hate in your mind, you do not get rid of it. Instead, you project it onto others. This does not end hate, it extends it. A self-talk statement like "I would never do that" is an example of projection. Instead of seeing your own hatefulness, you choose to see it in someone else. When you suppress or repress the hate in your mind, it's because you want to feel superior or better than someone else. The other person has to be bad so you can be "special" and good.

The only way to get rid of hate in your mind is to accept its presence. This enables you to neutralize it and then let it go. Acceptance doesn't have to be in the form of a gushing statement, a public confession, an apology, etc. It's just a quick and simple acknowledgement. Sort of like saying, "Okay, so what, I have hate in my mind." *Then express your willingness to let it go.* All that's needed is your tiny willingness. Give your hate to the Holy Spirit. He knows what to do with it. You don't.

> I notice I have hate in my mind. I recognize myself as a loving, harmless being through my willingness to forgive myself and through my willingness to give my hateful thoughts to the Holy Spirit. I love my little willingness, and I love myself.

Another challenge in dealing with hate is embracing the concept that all hate is equally destructive. This idea contradicts the messages we get in our daily lives. Society tells us that some hatefulness is okay and some isn't. Hatefulness is condoned or punished based on the degree of its severity and whether or not the hate is justified or legally mandated. A private hateful thought is okay. Hateful words may or may not be okay. Hateful actions might get you into legal trouble. Hate that physically maims is worse than hate that is emotionally painful. Hate that kills is worse than hate that maims. And so on. However, we experience guilt and do not feel good about ourselves anytime we are hateful.

This is because we are not recognizing or honoring our authentic Christ-self which only wants to be harmless and helpful to all. Ultimately, our ego-mind will inflict punishment for any form of hatefulness, no matter how seemingly small and insignificant.

As you can see, hateful thoughts have power because we give them power. They only "count" because we make them "count." The fastest and best way to deflate this power is to recognize that we don't know what hateful things mean. And if we do not know the meaning, then we cannot possibly judge in terms of goodness or badness. All we can do is witness and respond to what we are witnessing in the most harmless and uplifting way possible. The recognition that hateful thoughts have no meaning can be a turning point in your spiritual growth.

Why is the idea that hate has no meaning critically important?

🍃 There is no compromise. You either love or you don't. All expressions of hate are equally meaningless. All expressions of hate make you feel bad about yourself.

🍃 The ego likes to analyze and sensationalize hate. You can spend years trying to give hate meaning, but it is impossible to understand what has no meaning. Your Christ-self overlooks the meaningless, and uses every situation as inspiration to uplift.

- We cannot stop the hate that comes to our mind, but we do not have to keep it. We can change our minds, and we can tune out thoughts that come from the ego.

Radiant Meditation:

From lesson 243 in the Workbook   **ACIM-W.415**

Sit in silence with your eyes shut for at least a minute saying these words in your mind:

Today I will judge nothing that occurs.

Awaken Your Consciousness

A C T I V I T Y   # 1 0

Have you ever heard the saying "See no evil, hear no evil, speak no evil." The basic message is that even though you see something hateful, *you don't see it.* Even though you hear something hateful, *you don't hear it.* Even though you have hateful thoughts in your mind, you override them and *don't speak them.* This is a great reminder that anything that comes from hate is meaningless and should be treated as if it has no influence

Search your mind for thoughts that are distressing you. As each thought crosses your mind say,

My thought about _____ does not mean anything. ACIM-W.16

This will set your freedom from hate into motion.

Only you can save yourself

*Salvation is for the mind, and it is attained
through peace....Never lose sight of this, and
never allow yourself to believe, even for an instant,
that there is another answer.* **ACIM-T.221**

*...nothing outside yourself
can save you; nothing outside yourself
can give you peace...* **ACIM-W.119**

Salvation is not theoretical. **ACIM-M.65**

S anta Claus isn't coming to save you. The prince isn't
coming. The marines aren't coming either. Mom and
Dad might come for you, but they can't save you. Jesus and
other spiritual masters can teach you how to save yourself,
but none of them can save you **directly**. *You are the only one
who can save yourself, because you are the only one who has the*

power of decision. You decide what you will do or what you will refrain from doing. And as we've already discussed, every decision is an act of power.

But what is it that you're asked to decide?

- *Is it a decision about belief?* Do you have to believe in God? Or Jesus? Or Buddha? Or the Holy Spirit? Do you have to make a decision to join a specific church or group?
- *Is it a decision of action?* Should you attend church or temple more frequently? Should you participate in religious rituals or ceremonies? Should you pray more? Do more good deeds? Donate larger sums of money? Wear certain clothes, eat special foods, pledge allegiance to sacred symbols?

Do any of the decisions and activities that we normally associate with saving ourselves and getting into heaven actually work? Maybe. But then again, maybe not. The purpose of this discussion is to invite you to look more directly at what you're doing, or not doing, so that you can systematically assess your own personal effectiveness.

Many people base their beliefs about salvation on history. A history is a collection of stories, or "his story." Stories about God and salvation have been passed down for many thousands of years. Our parents had these ideas. Their parents had them. And so did countless generations that came before. These same ideas are taught today by respected, knowledgeable, and inspired religious leaders. If you go to a place of worship, it's highly likely that you will hear the same God story or a similar variation of the salvation theme. If you happen to listen to God programs on the TV or radio, these common ideas about God and salvation are the messages that will most likely be relayed. Many politicians hold these beliefs. So do celebrities. So do people who've achieved extraordinary success in life. So do our friends and neighbors. Everyone in our part of the universe, it seems, believes the stories that we have been taught about God and our eventual salvation.

With such overwhelming agreement, it simply does not occur to us to question the validity of the thought system upon which we base our lives and our deaths. Most of us take the path of least resistance. We embrace the ideas that have been passed down to us, and we walk the same path that millions have walked before us. But now you are being asked to consider a different perspective about salvation, and a different, less worn path.

To gain a new, non-religious perspective about the nature of salvation, you need to know what it means to save. When you save money, you're not spending it. You're putting it aside for another use later on. When you save or store food, you're not eating it. You're putting it aside for another use later on. When you save stamps, or comic books, or other collectibles, you're not using them. You're putting them aside to accumulate value. **The primary characteristic of saving is not spending or not using something.** Therefore, when you save yourself, you have to not do something. Or said another way, instead of spending your life-energy, you save it. Life-energy is always saved through the practice of inner peace. This is why inner peace is a cornerstone of God's plan.

Of course, to stay alive and to be alive, we cannot always be in a state of energy conservation. We cannot always be completely still and at peace. *The big secret is to only use your life-energy in a conscious, constructive way that's in accord with God's Will.* This prevents mistakes and enables you to always feel good about yourself and to *always* be happy. When life-energy is spent unconsciously or on mistakes, you feel bad about yourself. The bad feeling isn't because you're a bad person or for moral reasons. It's because you've used your life-energy on something that has no meaning, no use, no value. The word *devil* is a derivative of the Greek word *diabolos*, which means good for nothing. Whenever you engage in diabolical thoughts or behavior, you'll automatically feel bad about yourself because you're *wasting* your life-energy on something that's good for nothing.

God's plan for salvation *saves* you from experiencing the two diabolical emotions of anger and guilt, which are both good for nothing. We already know that anger is hate expressed outwards to another, and that guilt is hate expressed inwards to the self. Anger is always self-destructive because no matter how much the anger may seem justified, it *always* produces guilt. Guilt results in a loss of happiness, suf-fering of every kind, self-inflicted punishment, sickness, and ultimately death. *God wants to save you from this useless misery.* **God wills you to be happy!**

The Course gives you a strategy and two powerful tools for saving yourself from this waste of life-energy. *The strategy is to turn every hateful, conflicted relationship into a holy relationship.* Everyone has a difficult relationship with someone. Let that difficult person be the one who inspires you to learn about peace, goodness, and love. We prefer to think that inspiration comes from a book or a classroom or a spiritual vision. It's exasperating to realize that the best inspiration comes from the people in our lives who push our buttons and make us crazy. These people are of great value because they rile and provoke us to make a conscious choice for love, and they do it over, and over, and over again! This is actually the fastest and most efficient way to learn how to "be love."

The two tools were discussed previously. One is the *holy instant,* a moment of peace which prevents anger or guilt from occurring. The other is *forgiveness,* a harmless way to acknowledge and neutralize anger or guilt once it appears. There's a mistaken belief that forgiveness is something you do once or twice or maybe even a handful of times, and then you're done with it. But this will not result in spiritual fitness, and it will not bring about the transformation of self that you seek.

Compare your spiritual fitness to the time and effort it takes to achieve physical fitness. If, for example, your goal is to build large muscles in your upper arms, you would have to do at least 8 to 12 repetitions of an arm-curl exercise at least 3 times per week for several weeks. That's 24 repetitions per week to make a big, beautiful muscle. The same kind of rigorous training program is needed to re-discover your big, beautiful Christ-self. This is not to suggest that you should forgive a predefined number of times each week or that you turn forgiveness into an exercise ritual! It's simply to make the point that *forgiveness needs to be a regular and rigorous ongoing part of your daily life, like brushing your teeth.* We all value clean teeth and a clean house, but we pay little attention to having a clean mind. It's very hard to be happy when you're walking in garbage, living in garbage, and wallowing in garbage. The only way to be happy is to get rid of the garbage. This is what forgiveness does for you. It gets rid of the hateful garbage you carry around in your mind.

When hate is removed from your mind, your mind is holy. The word *holy* is related to the word *halo*. A halo is a circle of light around the head, which is where your mind is located. Only the mind can be light or dark. Darkness is the symbol for the presence of hate. Light is the symbol for the absence of hate. Whenever you see the word *halo* or a derivative of the word *halo*, think in terms of light or absence of hate.

> *Our Father, who art in Heaven, hallowed be thy name*
> becomes
> *Our Father, who art in Heaven, light be thy name.*

When you make the decision to undo the darkness in your own mind, your mind becomes holy. Holy is also related to the word *whole*. When your mind has hate in it, it's separated from God. A thing that is in separate parts cannot be whole. When your mind is free of hate, it's joined with God and with your brothers and sisters. Union is wholeness. The expression "what God has joined, let no man put asunder" refers to the joining of minds, not of physical bodies. Lastly, holy is related to the word *heal*. Healing seems like a physical process, but it's really an undoing of an unloving error in the mind. When the mind is healed, the body automatically follows suit. In all cases, holiness is *of* God, and when your mind is free of hate, it is aligned with His. Therefore, *your salvation is directly linked to your willingness and ability to free your mind of hate.*

Remember:

- Only you can save yourself, because only you can make the decision to remove hate from your mind and to be at peace. God's plan for salvation is the undoing of hate.

- Peace saves your life-energy. Anger and guilt waste it.

- A moment of peace enables you to connect with your Christ-self and make a decision about how to progress that leaves you feeling good about yourself and others. Forgiveness enables you to restore peace when it has been disturbed.

Becoming Holy
AN EXERCISE IN SALVATION

We owe gratitude to our fellow brothers and sisters who bring us inspiration in the form of difficult or challenging relationships. In these situations, you're not expected to let your problems with others go unresolved, to suffer in silence, or to sacrifice yourself. Instead, you are asked to see the goodness in these people and to solve your problems in the most harmless and uplifting way possible.

Act now on the inspiration from another to turbo-charge your Christ-self conscious awareness and to be holy. Think of someone you don't like or who you are holding a grudge against. What are the specific things that bother you about this person? List each little thing that disturbs your peace.

- I am disturbed because Jennifer doesn't pay enough attention to me.
- I am disturbed because Jennifer is messy.
- I am disturbed because Jennifer sometimes says unkind things.
- I am disturbed because Jennifer is not spiritually aware.
- I am disturbed because Jennifer is unfair.
- And so on.

Don't judge yourself as wrong or bad for having these thoughts. The first step is to consciously acknowledge that you have them. This is how you recognize the problem. The second step is to remember you are love. Instead of indulging yourself and allowing your loveless thoughts to continue, you change your mind. Whenever you deliberately override an unloving thought with a loving one, you are changing your mind. This simple change of mind enables you to see your Christ-self. What could be more important or more useful than witnessing yourself as a loving being? Your Christ-self shines through every time a loveless thought is undone. And finally, the third step is to turn everything over to the Holy Spirit, with no strings attached. The Holy Spirit knows how to use all situations for good. You do not. Let the Holy Spirit determine the result.

Say to yourself:

God is the Love in which I forgive _____.   *ACIM.W-73*

There is nothing my holiness cannot do.   *ACIM-W.58*

My holiness blesses _____.   *ACIM-W.56*

A formless role model

I am your model for decision.
By deciding for God, I showed you
that this decision can be made,
and that you can make it. **ACIM-T.77**

You are the light of the world with me.
Rest does not come from sleeping
but from waking. **ACIM-T.77**

I do not call for martyrs
but for teachers. **ACIM-T.95**

here are basically two ways to learn how to do things.
We can teach ourselves through trial and error, or we
can learn from someone who's already successfully figured it out.
We're all intimately familiar with the trial-and-error technique. Yes, it may eventually produce the intended result,

but trial and error is also time-consuming, frustrating, usually painful, and frequently leads to a dead end. The fastest, most efficient, most inspiring way to learn something is to follow the lead of a bona fide role model. The role model demonstrates what you're supposed to do and how you're supposed to do it. This is the whole rationale behind thousands of how-to books, audio tapes, and video instruction cassettes. It's why we pay attention to extraordinary business leaders and great parents.

But who has grown to the point where no further spiritual growth is necessary? Where do we go to find a how-to demonstration of formlessness? Who among us is awake? Who can be our mentor, our guide? Not surprisingly, the answer is Jesus. A Jesus who is mystical, radiant, radical, and available to all. This is how He comes to us through *A Course In Miracles*®. As you might predict, Jesus uses the Course to lead us to love. But he leads in an unconventional way. For one thing, Jesus is wholly free of a connection to any religion or any organized group. For another, He teaches independence from rituals and reliance on anything external. And most importantly, Jesus does not come to us in person. He comes to us as a formless, loving presence with the most uplifting and beautiful ideas imaginable.

Most of us recognize Jesus through his physical form. We've seen pictures and sculptures of a slim man with a fair complexion, long hair, refined features, and biblical-style clothing. Oftentimes the images show him suffering on a cross. But in the Course, Jesus does not present himself with this familiar image. In fact, he comes with no form at all. How, then, can we recognize him? How can we be absolutely sure it's *Him* without any hesitation or doubt? How would we *know*?

There are many clues that lead us to believe the Course is authored by Jesus:

- We would recognize Jesus today exactly as we would recognize Him during his earthly life, as a wholly benign and radiantly loving presence. The only difference is that his presence is no longer dependent on or limited by a body.

- We would recognize Jesus today exactly as we would have recognized Him during his earthly life, by the magnificent ideas that he teaches. Because Jesus is free of the ego, his ideas are pure love, consistently logical, extraordinarily beautiful, and highly magnetic. They are the call to joy that you so long to answer.

- We would recognize Jesus today exactly as we would have recognized Him during his earthly life, because he is the shining role model of what we all must come to be. He is love, only love, always love.

- We would recognize Jesus today exactly as we would have recognized Him during his earthly life, as an equal elder brother, not a lord to be worshipped and idolized. This is tremendously useful to us because if Jesus can live without specialness, then so can we.

◉ We would recognize Jesus today exactly as we would have recognized Him during his earthly life, as the one who inspires us to think the highest thoughts of ourselves and others. He speaks of your holiness, your ability to heal yourself and others, your role in God's plan for salvation. He inspires you to be *of* Him and teach with Him.

It's no accident that Jesus comes to us through the Course in a formless way. It is intentional and on purpose. He makes formlessness real. He makes it doable. He makes it attractive. If Jesus did not serve as a formless beacon, how else could we muster up the interest and the willingness to become formless ourselves? Form is simply not necessary in the real world, the world we cannot see. It's only needed here in the earthly world that we made up.

Since we are not yet in the real world, Jesus uses a book to convey his magnificent ideas. People with minds that are blocked temporarily need an easily understandable, accessible, and non-threatening tool to develop their spiritual abilities. The Course teaches us how to commune with the Holy Spirit that resides within. It teaches reliance on spiritual vision, instead of human perception. It teaches how to consciously decide to be love, instead of an ego predator. And it teaches how to use peace to join with God and your brothers. Yes, you can get the lessons elsewhere, but why continue seeking when the perfect Source of Love is as close as the nearest bookstore or e-commerce outlet.

The most enjoyable aspect of the Course is that it enables you to meet your role model for formless spiritual growth in a direct and personal way. When you read the Course or Workbook exercises, it *feels* like you have a one-on-one relationship with Jesus, and this is immensely pleasing. He provides a clear roadmap for getting your feet up out of the gutter and onto another plane. And even more important, he provides the inspiration to actually do it. There are no specific rules, only general guidelines. The guidelines lift you up, they renew you, and they revitalize you. They enable you to see yourself and your role in the world in a new and glorious way.

Here's a sample. Read the following ideas and see for yourself if they have the power to move you in a brilliant new direction. Read them and see for yourself if the source is Love.

There is nothing about me that you cannot attain.
I have nothing that does not come from God.
The difference between us now
is that I have nothing else. **ACIM-T.7**

(In reference to the crucifixion) I elected,
for your sake and mine, to demonstrate
that the most outrageous assault, as judged
by the ego, does not matter. **ACIM-T.93**

You are asked to live so as to demonstrate
that you are not an ego, and I do not choose
God's channels wrongly. **ACIM-T.68.**

*Your gratitude to your brother is
the only gift I want.* **ACIM-T.69**

*Teach peace with me and stand
with me on holy ground.* **ACIM-T.284**

*You can do anything I ask.
I have asked you to perform miracles
and have made it clear that miracles are natural,
corrective, healing, and universal.* **ACIM-T.19**

*My birth in you is your awakening to grandeur.
Welcome me not into a manger,
but into the altar to holiness, where holiness
abides in perfect peace.* **ACIM-T.308**

*...those who accept me as a model
are literally my disciples. Disciples are followers,
and if the model they follow has chosen
to save them pain in all respects, they are
unwise not to follow him.* **ACIM-T.93**

*The power of one mind can shine
into another, because all the lamps of God
were lit by the same spark. It is everywhere
and it is eternal.* **ACIM-T.175**

The Course invites you to shine like
the beacon of light that you are.

Be love now

*Your task is not to seek for love, but merely
to seek and find all of the barriers within yourself
that you have built against it.* **ACIM–T.338**

*Every loveless thought must
be undone.* **ACIM–T.87**

ear ones,

Spiritual ideas don't work unless you use them. This concept might be compared to reading a diet book, but not following up by doing something with the information. That type of dieter might know a lot about how to take off weight yet understand nothing about the experience of being thin. A similar principle applies to what you just read here. Knowing about forgiveness is not the same thing as actually forgiving. Knowing about tapping into your Inner Teacher for guidance is not the same thing as receiving guidance and applying it. Knowing that God is love is not the same as feeling personally connected to God through your own direct experience of love. See what I mean? You can't just read about it and feel all smug and smart. You have to put the ideas into practice to get the remarkable effect.

Please don't wait another minute for love to come into your life experience. Start today. Be love now. This very minute! Don't wait for the perfect conditions in your life. They don't exist. Don't wait for the perfect people to present themselves. They aren't coming. Be the love you are. This is the only thing that's really important.

Consider responding to a sincere invitation from me to you: *Please send me a love letter.* It should be a love letter with a very, very big heart. Tell me how *being love* has changed your life. I will patiently wait to hear from you.

Here's how to reach me:

Karen Bentley
BIG HEART

E-MAIL: info@big-heart.com
U.S. MAIL: P.O. Box 909, Sudbury, MA 01776

The Lord's Prayer

Our Father,
> We are the indistinguishable children of one creator.

Who art in heaven
> Our creator's home is not the world we see. There is another world we don't see.

Hallowed be thy name
> God's name is love and only love.

Thy kingdom come
> We will all return home to the real world,

Thy Will be done
> When we ask God's Will in every decision.

On earth as it is in Heaven
> Heaven and earth are indistinguishable whenever we experience peace, love, and joy.

Give us this day
> We only know life in the present moment.
> The past and the future do not exist.

Our daily bread
> Let us learn that we need but ask for what we want to receive it.

And forgive us our trespasses
> We know that you overlook and do not see our mistakes.

As we forgive those who trespass against us
And so we overlook the mistakes of others.

And lead us not into temptation
Your peace will save us from all mistakes and will guide our thoughts and actions.

But deliver us from evil
When you lead us to make the choice for love instead of hate.

For thine is the kingdom, the power, and the glory, now and forever.
Death is not real because we share your eternal power and eternal life and eternal glory forever.

Amen.

APPENDIX A:

A Course In Miracles® web sites

Foundation for A Course In Miracles
Institute, retreat center, copyright permission
    Newsletter: *The Lighthouse*
    Location: Temecula, California
www.facim.org

Foundation for Inner Peace
Original publisher/distributor
ACIM translation program
    Location: Tiburon, California
www.acim.org

Miracle Distribution Center
Worldwide contact point for ACIM and educational center
Maintains accurate study group listings
ACIM booksore
    Newsletter: *The Holy Encounter*
    Location: Fullerton, California
www.miraclecenter.org

Pathways of Light

Educational and correspondence programs
Facilitator/ministry training

Location: Kiel, Wisconsin

www.pathwaysoflight.org

Community Miracles Center

Community educational/fellowship center
ACIM booksore

Newsletter: Miracles Monthly

Location: San Francisco, CA

www.miracles-course.org

Circle of Atonement

Teaching and healing center

Newsletter: A Better Way

Location: Sedona, AZ

http://nen.sedona.net/circleofa/

Quest Foundation

New England-based support network for ACIM study groups
Quest Center for Attitudinal Healing

Newsletter: The Spirit's Voice

www.QuestFoundation.org

Northwest Foundation for A Course In Miracles

Site to connect with Raj a/k/a Paul Tuttle

Newsletter: *Conversations with Raj*

Location: Kingston, Washington

www.nwffacim.org

Authors who write about the Course

Tom Carpenter
Dialogue on Awakening

Paul Ferrini
Reflections on the Christ Mind
Love Without Conditions
The Bridge to Reality
www.dap.nl/Ferrini.htm

Jacob Glass
Invocations
http://members.aol.com/jaket36/

Brent Haskell
Journey Beyond Words
The Other Voice
www.windhorse.org/brent_haskell.html

Carol Howe

Healing the Hurt Behind Addictions
Homeward to an Open Door
www.carolhowe.com

Gerald Jampolsky, MD

Love Is Letting Go of Fear
Forgiveness: The Greatest Healer of All
Love Is the Answer: Creating Positive Relationships
Teach Only Love: The 12 Principles of Attitudinal Healing
Change Your Mind, Change Your Life
Out of Darkness into the Light
Attaining Inner Peace
Mini Course
Good-bye to Guilt
www.healingcenter.org
www.spiritwalk.org

Andrew LeCompte

Creating Harmonious Relationships
www.letstalk.org

D. Patrick Miller

The Complete Story of the Course
A Little Book of Forgiveness
The Book of Practical Faith
www.fearlesbooks.com

Jon Mundy

Awaken To Your Own Call: Exploring A Course In Miracles
The Ten Laws of Happiness
Listening to Your Inner Guide
www.interfaithfellowship.org

Robert Perry

An Introduction to ACIM
Relationships as a Spiritual Journey
http://nen.sedona.net/circleofa/

Robert Skutch

Journey Without Distance

Kenneth Wapnick

Absense from Felicity
The Fifty Miracles Principles of ACIM
Love Does Not Condemn
A Course In Miracles and Christianity
The Obstacles to Peace
Glossary Index for ACIM
www.facim.org

Allen Watson

A Workbook Companion, Volumes I, II, III
http://nen.sedona.net/circleofa/

Marrianne Williamson

A Return to Love

Illuminata

Emma and Mommy Talk to God

www.marianne.com

*When your body and your ego and
your dreams are gone,
you will know that you will last forever.*

*Perhaps you think this is accomplished
through death,
but nothing is accomplished through death,
because death is nothing.*

*Everything is accomplished through life,
and life is of the mind and in the mind.*

*The body neither lives nor dies,
because it cannot contain you who are life.*

*If we share the same mind,
you can overcome death because I did.*

ACIM-T.104